INSIGHTS

VIKINGS

FIONA MACDONALD

INSIGHTS

VIKINGS

FIONA MACDONALD

A QUARTO BOOK

First edition for the United States and Canada published
1993 by Barron's Educational Series, Inc.

Copyright © 1992 Quarto Publishing plc

All inquiries should be addressed to:
Barron's Educational Series, Inc.
250 Wireless Boulevard
Hauppauge, New York 11788

Library of Congress Catalog Card No. 93-16416

International Standard Book No. 0-8120-6375-9

Library of Congress Cataloging-in-Publication Data

Macdonald, Fiona.
    Vikings / Fiona Macdonald. — 1st ed. for the United States and Canada.
        p.   cm. — (Insights)
    Includes index.
    Summary: Examines the history, culture, daily life, and explorations of
the Vikings.
        ISBN 0-8120-6375-9
        1. Vikings—Juvenile literature.   2. Northmen—Juvenile literature. [1. Vikings]
I. Title.   II. Series: Insights (Barron's Educational Series, Inc.)
DL65.M29   1993
948'.022—dc20   93-16416
                                                                              CIP
                                                                              AC

This book was designed and produced by
Quarto Publishing plc
The Old Brewery, 6 Blundell Street, London N7 9BH

Consultant Dr. Sue Margeson

Art Director Nick Buzzard

Senior Editor Kate Scarborough
Editor Alison Murdoch
Designer Steve Wilson
Illustrators Sharon Smith, Jim Robins
Picture Researcher Louise Edgeworth

The Publishers would like to thank the following for their help in the
preparation of this book: Karen Ball, Trish Going, and Marcus Bell

Picture Acknowledgments Key: a = above, b = below, l = left, r = right,
c = center

Quarto would like to thank the following for providing photographs and for
permission to reproduce copyright material. While every effort has been made
to trace and acknowledge all copyright holders, we would like to apologize
should any omissions have been made.

ATA Archive; pages 26br, 43bl, 51br; CM Dixon; pages 10ar, 13cl, 14cr, 15al, 17cr, 18bc,
19br, 21cl, 22bl, 24b, 24cr, 26ar, 27bl, 29al, 29ar, 32al, 35bl, 38b, 40bl, 42cr, 42ar, 43ar,
44ar, 44br, 45br, 46ar, 46b, 47cl, 47br, 48bl, 49al, 50bl, 50cr, 51ar; Niels Elswing, pages
23l, 40ar; McQuitty International, pages 17ar, 21al; Mick Sharp, pages 12c, 13bl, 18br,
34cr, 45al; (Archives of) the Swedish Central Board of National Antiquities, pages 10bl,
11al, 14ar, 15ac, 23br, 38ar, 44bl; Trip, pages 10cr, 18bl, 30cr, 49al, 51bl; York Archaeological
Trust, pages 12cl, 13ar, 15ar, 21ar, 22br, 25cr, 25br, 28br, 33cl, 35cr, 36cr,
39ar, 39bl, 39br, 39cr, 41a, 42bl, 43al.

Manufactured in Singapore by Eray Scan Pte Ltd
Printed in Singapore by Star Standard Industries (Pte) Ltd

3456   987654321

CONTENTS

WHO WERE THE VIKINGS?

When you read the word "Vikings," what pictures come into your mind? Brave, well-armed warriors? Ruthless pirates and raiders? Quarrelsome, boastful, dangerous men, fiercely loyal to their leaders but bringing death and destruction to everyone else? These warlike images are well known. But, however exciting, they tell us about only a small part of Viking life.

Some Vikings did spend their time raiding and fighting, but the majority of Viking men and women lived peacefully at home, working hard to make a living from their lands, or to find a market for the goods they had produced. The Vikings lived in northern Europe, in the present-day countries of Norway, Denmark, and Sweden. Their ancestors

▶ **Checkmate?**
This chess piece, made of walrus ivory, dates from the very end of the time when Viking states were powerful, around AD 1200. It was discovered on the island of Lewis, off the Scottish coast. The Vikings enjoyed board games.

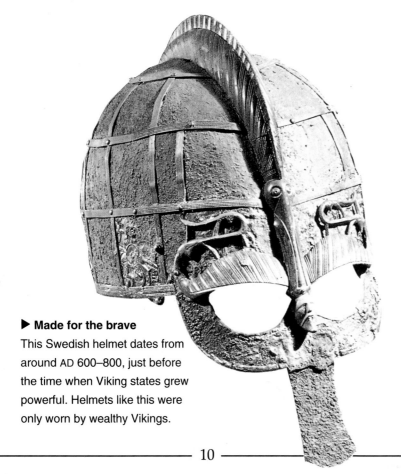

▶ **Made for the brave**
This Swedish helmet dates from around AD 600–800, just before the time when Viking states grew powerful. Helmets like this were only worn by wealthy Vikings.

▲ **What's in a name?**
Viking pirates were known by several different names, including "men from the north" and "raiders." No one is certain where the name "Viking" comes from. Some scholars think it originated in the Vikings' own word—"vik"—for a sheltered, deep-water bay, where raiders could keep their ships. Today, these viks are called *fjords*; this one is in Norway.

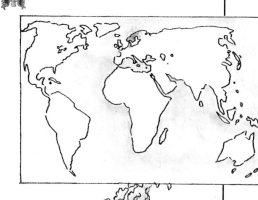

▶ **Viking homelands**

The ancestors of the Vikings had lived in the Scandinavian lands of Norway, Sweden, and Denmark for many hundreds of years before the Viking people grew strong enough to make raids, win battles, and make new settlements in other parts of Europe. This Viking expansion began around AD 800 and continued until around AD 1100.

☐ Danish Vikings

☐ Norwegian Vikings

☐ Swedish Vikings

had been settled there for centuries, but between AD 800 and 1100 the Viking peoples grew powerful. They established strong towns and grew rich through trade. They designed sleek ships, and sailed across oceans to settle in distant lands.

Viking lives

The Vikings were farmers, fishermen, trappers, and traders. Viking craftsmen made beautiful objects out of wood, metal, and bone; Viking women were skillful weavers, and produced fine, warm textiles. All free adult men had a say in how their community was run; traces of this early Viking democracy still influence local government in many lands today. Viking poets, known as *skalds*, recorded all these achievements in their verses.

The Vikings lived at a time when most people could not read or write, so documents describing their activities are rare. They also lived when warfare—and the destruction that went with it—was common. Much Viking evidence has therefore been lost. Viking settlements were widely spaced in the countryside, so isolated sites may still be undiscovered. And in towns, important Viking evidence has been, until recently, buried deep below roads, houses, and office buildings.

Viking remains

In spite of all these problems, archaeologists and historians have been able to discover a great deal about Viking life. The evidence they have comes from several sources—stone monuments, graves, hidden treasures, accidental finds, and carefully planned excavations. Many fine examples of Viking metalwork and carving have survived, as well as huge earthworks, abandoned towns, and the ruins of Viking buildings.

Preserved underwater

Viking clothes were made of materials like wool and leather. Viking boats, and many Viking homes, were built of wood. These are all perishable; many have rotted way, but a few have been preserved underwater or in damp, marshy ground. From the remains of Viking ships raised from the seabed, archaeologists have been able to reconstruct their shapes and sizes (see pages 16–17). Excavations in

▲ **Preserved in stone**
Carvings like this fragment from a memorial at Chester-le-Street, in the north of England, provide us with evidence about Viking weapons and warfare.

▶ **Viking site**
Remains of a Viking farmstead at Jarlshof, Sumburgh, in the Shetland Islands. Excavations have shown that the site was occupied from the ninth through the eleventh centuries, and that many improvements and additions were made to the original house.

waterlogged soil, like those at York, England, have revealed the walls of wooden houses, along with boots, shoes, socks, weapons, armor, and fragments of clothing.

Viking words

Viking beliefs and traditions are preserved in songs and poems, and in sagas—long family histories and adventure stories dating from the twelfth and thirteenth centuries. There are also Viking law-codes and runic inscriptions that record important events. Peoples who were attacked by the Vikings, or who traveled to their lands, also wrote down their own observations and opinions of Viking life.

▶ Life story
Memorial stone carved with *runes* (Viking letters) from Uppland, Sweden. The writing says: "Estrid had this stone carved in memory of Osten her husband who went to Jerusalem and died in Greece."

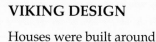

▼ Ancient memories
Remains of a twelfth-century stone fort at Cubbie Roo's Castle, Wyre, in the Orkney Islands.

▼ Under the ash
As they cleared away the thick layers of ash, the archaeologists realized that they had discovered an important Viking site. In Stong Valley, Iceland, they found the remains of a complete farmstead, very well preserved. They used these remains to build a modern copy, or reconstruction, of the farm as it appeared in late Viking times.

The main building at Stong was the farmhouse, where the farmer lived with his family. It was divided into several large rooms. The hall, probably used for sleeping and for entertaining, was over 40 feet (12 m) long. There was also a living room, where the women of the household sat and did their spinning; a dairy, with vats for storing milk and a stone *quern* (simple hand-powered machine) for grinding corn; and a lavatory. Outside was a cattle shed, a smithy (blacksmith's workshop), and a barn.

VIKING DESIGN

Houses were built around a timber frame, which was covered by logs, or (as here) by turf. The walls were lined with wooden planks. There might be a central fireplace, to keep the house warm.

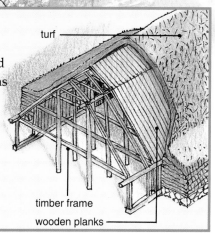

turf

timber frame

wooden planks

▲ Buried by a volcano

Iceland is a cold region, but it also has many active volcanoes, steaming lakes, and hot springs. For this reason, it is often called "the land of fire and ice." In AD 1104, the volcano Mount Hekla erupted. A large area was covered several yards deep in volcanic ash. Everything there was hidden for hundreds of years, until, in 1939, a team of archaeologists decided to investigate…

INTERNATIONAL TRADE

Life in the Viking homelands was tough. If a young man had no land, no craft skills, and did not want to risk his neck in a Viking ship, what could he do? If he had energy and intelligence, he might still hope to make his fortune through international trade.

Viking trade routes stretched from Ireland in the west to Baghdad and Constantinople in the east. There, they joined the intercontinental trading highways—the "Silk Route" and the "Spice Route"—which linked Europe to India, Central Asia, and China. It could take a year to make a one-way journey like this so it was only worthwhile if you had valuable goods to sell. Exotic, imported treasures from many lands have been found at Viking sites, and Viking products have been unearthed at trading towns in Europe and the Mediterranean lands. The Vikings preferred to barter, although they sometimes paid with coins.

Trade in Russia

Viking traders covered enormous distances in search of wealth. But they were not the only travelers. Merchants from the rich cities of the Middle East made their way through snowbound forests and along frozen rivers to Viking trading posts. There, they exchanged silks, spices, wine, and silver for slaves, furs, honey, and wax.

Viking merchants handled a great deal of Russian trade, and helped to establish important cities at Novgorod, Staraja Ladoga, and Kiev. Viking traders also sold prisoners, iron, amber, weapons and the whetstones for sharpening them, soapstone cooking pots, hides, furs, and walrus ivory.

▶ German glass

A delicate glass beaker (upside down), made in the Rhineland and found at the important Swedish trading town of Birka. It must have been brought there by merchants.

▲ Buried treasure

This hoard of silver was found in the grave of a rich Viking buried in Sweden during the tenth century. It also contains money from different parts of Europe, and solid silver coins patterned with Arabic writing, which were made in Muslim lands. Evidence like this tells us that there were trading contacts between Vikings and Muslims at this time.

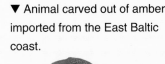

▼ Animal carved out of amber imported from the East Baltic coast.

▼ Warm-water shell, brought from the Middle East and used in making jewelry.

▲ Decorated glass egg, a Christian Easter symbol, brought from Russia.

GOODS FROM MANY LANDS

All kinds of exotic objects have been found in Viking graves. They tell us about the Viking people's love of fine things. They tell us, too, that some Vikings were rich enough to purchase these very expensive imported foreign luxuries.

▶ **Long-distance trade**
Viking merchants traveled throughout Europe and ventured eastward across Russia, to the great trading cities of the Middle East. There, they struck bargains with other merchants arriving from as far away as India and China.

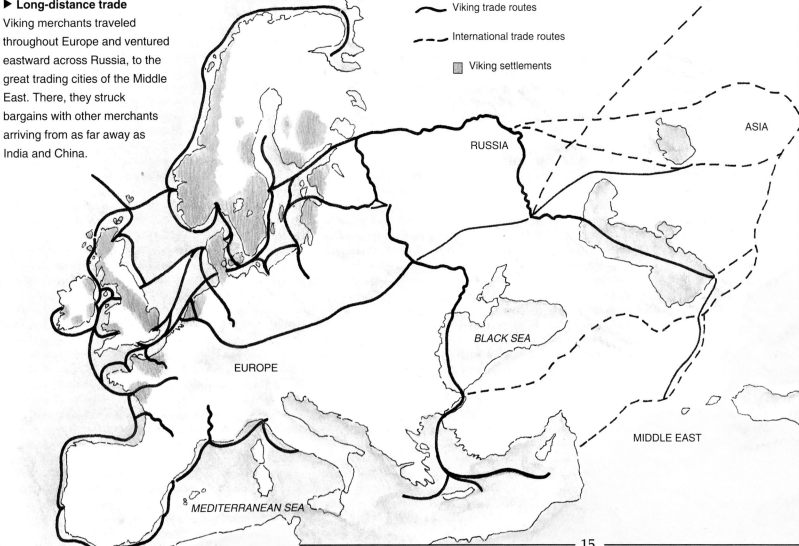

—— Viking trade routes

- - - International trade routes

▨ Viking settlements

ASIA

RUSSIA

BLACK SEA

EUROPE

MIDDLE EAST

MEDITERRANEAN SEA

VIKING SHIPS

Viking trade, settlements overseas, or even raids, would not have been possible without good ships. Before Viking times, the peoples of Scandinavia had built sturdy boats, but these do not compare for speed, size, or seaworthiness, with the strong and graceful ships designed by craftsmen between AD 800–1100.

▲ **Men at work**
Down by the water's edge, the men are busy. The air is full of the sounds of sawing and hammering, mingled with shouts from the foreman and the thunder of waves crashing on the rocky shore. The master fusses around, checking everyone's work—and making complaints. What is the reason for all this activity?

▼ **Riding the waves**
The Vikings were proud of their ships, and showed great bravery in setting sail across the rough northern ocean. The names Vikings chose for their ships record this fierce pride: *Long Serpent*, *Dragon*, and *Wave-Strider*.

Viking ships were built of wood. The hulls were made of overlapping planks, fastened to a strong wooden keel. Each plank was about an inch (2.5 cm) thick. They were nailed together, and a thick wadding of moss or tarred wool was used to fill any cracks. There was a single mast, which carried a large, square sail. In calm weather, or when close to land, ships could also be rowed with oars.

Viking craftsmen did not use plans or drawings to help them; they were guided by tradition and

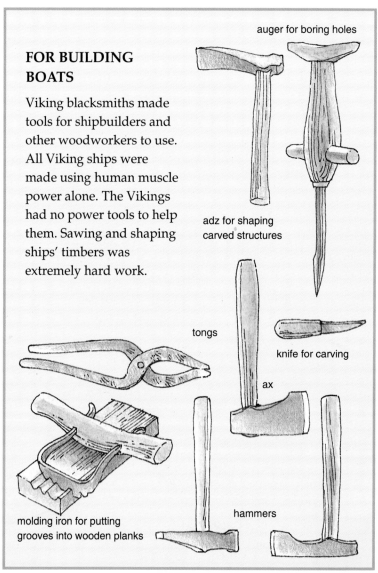

FOR BUILDING BOATS

Viking blacksmiths made tools for shipbuilders and other woodworkers to use. All Viking ships were made using human muscle power alone. The Vikings had no power tools to help them. Sawing and shaping ships' timbers was extremely hard work.

auger for boring holes

adz for shaping carved structures

tongs

knife for carving

ax

hammers

molding iron for putting grooves into wooden planks

by their own judgment and experience. Ships varied in size, depending on how they were to be used. They were often given names, and decorated with ferocious or fanciful creatures carved on prows and sterns.

Sailing and steering

The remains of several Viking ships have survived. From them, archaeologists have discovered how ships were built and how they might have been sailed. Modern reconstructions, based on these remains, reveal that Viking ships were well designed to survive stormy northern seas. They were light and flexible, riding over the waves rather than fighting through them. They were also easy to steer, fast (about eight miles per hour [13 kmph] when rowed) and surprisingly watertight. Viking sailors steered using an oar at the stern of the ship. They set a course by observing the stars and

▶ Sailing home
Carvings like this provide us with valuable evidence about Viking ships' sails and rigging, which have long since rotted away.

▼ Snarling beast
Carved wooden heads, like this sea monster from Norway, were used to decorate the richest Viking ships.

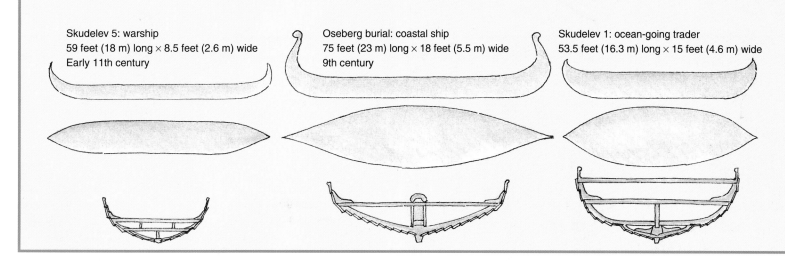

SHIP DESIGN

Our knowledge of Viking ships comes mostly from remains of wooden hulls that have been preserved in deep water and mud off the Scandinavian coast, and from ship-burials, where the wood has been preserved by damp soil.

These survivals tell us several things: that Viking ships varied widely in shape and size; that different Viking ships were designed to be suitable for different purposes; and that Viking ships were strong and extremely well made.

Skudelev 5: warship
59 feet (18 m) long × 8.5 feet (2.6 m) wide
Early 11th century

Oseberg burial: coastal ship
75 feet (23 m) long × 18 feet (5.5 m) wide
9th century

Skudelev 1: ocean-going trader
53.5 feet (16.3 m) long × 15 feet (4.6 m) wide

natural patterns like the flight of birds, floating ice, or, when nearing land, the smell of sheep.

From the early ninth century onward, Viking sailors traveled to distant lands. Their journeys were long, cold, wet, crowded, uncomfortable, and often dangerous. For example, the sagas tell us that of the 25 ships that sailed from Iceland to Greenland in AD 985, hoping to set up a new colony, only 14 arrived. The others had to turn back, or were lost at sea.

Leaving home

So why did the Vikings travel? We have seen how some Viking merchants journeyed for trade. Other Vikings went in search of loot, as you can read on pages 20–21. But they were a minority. Most Vikings traveled in search of somewhere better to live. They wanted to get away from the cold weather, poor soils, and bad harvests of their homelands. Some later settlers also wanted to escape from the increasing pressure of people in the Viking homelands, or from the growing strength and authority of Viking kings.

The earliest Viking settlers migrated to the Orkneys and Shetlands, the Isle of Man, Scotland, and Ireland. They captured the local farmers and made them work as slaves. Vikings also settled in the Faeroe Islands, where they drove out the monks who had gone there in search of peace.

They ventured farther, to Iceland in 874 and to Greenland in 985, where they established settlements. They even crossed the Atlantic Ocean to reach the coast of Newfoundland (in present-day Canada) almost 500 years before Christopher Columbus made his famous "discovery" of the American New World.

HISTORIC HOMES

Skafjord, Iceland, was where Thorfinn Karlsefni, one of the first Vikings to travel to North America, chose to settle when he returned home safely to Iceland after his historic voyage. Karlsefni's original house has not survived, but it was almost certainly single-storied and turf-covered.

◄ ▼ The Vikings were here
There is evidence of Viking settlements in many northern European lands. Left: Viking cross was found at Middleton, in Yorkshire. Below: site of a Viking burial at Kingscross Point on the Isle of Arran.

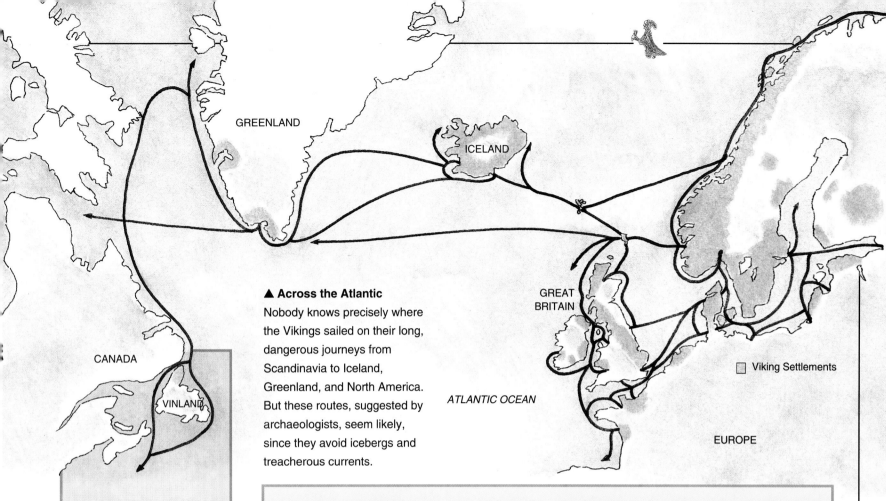

GREENLAND

ICELAND

GREAT
BRITAIN

CANADA

VINLAND

▲ Across the Atlantic

Nobody knows precisely where the Vikings sailed on their long, dangerous journeys from Scandinavia to Iceland, Greenland, and North America. But these routes, suggested by archaeologists, seem likely, since they avoid icebergs and treacherous currents.

ATLANTIC OCEAN

☐ Viking Settlements

EUROPE

VINLAND

In AD 987 Bjarni Herjolfsson was blown off course and sighted North America. His sightings interested another Viking sailor, Leif Eriksson. In 1002, he landed in Newfoundland and spent the winter there. He called the place Vinland (Wineland), because he saw wild grapes growing. Leif returned home to share the news. Soon, other Vikings sailed for Vinland, intending to settle there. But after three winters, the Vikings left.

A VIKING CANAL

Viking sailors needed safe anchorages for their boats during wild northern winters. Sometimes they built simple harbors, but they were not strong enough to withstand the fierce Atlantic waves off the west coast of Scotland. So the Vikings dug this canal at Ruadha´dunain, from the sea to a small *loch* (lake) inland. Their boats could shelter safely there, without being smashed against the rocks on the beach.

RAIDERS FROM THE SEA

In 793, the English scholar Alcuin sent a hurried letter to the King of Northumbria. He was reporting a horrifying event—the first Viking raid on Britain. "Never before," he wrote "has such terror appeared in Britain as we have now suffered… nor was it thought that such an inroad from the sea could be made. Behold, the Church of St. Cuthbert spattered with the blood of the priests of God."

The Viking attack on St. Cuthbert Church—part of the famous monastery at Lindisfarne, an island off the Northumbrian coast—was soon repeated elsewhere. For the next 300 years, people living along the coasts of Britain, France, and the Baltic countries went in fear of Viking attack. They watched the horizon anxiously for signs of the swift Viking ships—like evil black birds, as one French chronicler described them. Only stormy weather kept them safe. An Irish monk wrote, "The wind is rough tonight, tossing the white hair of the ocean. I do not fear the fierce Vikings, racing across the sea."

▶ **Howling warriors**
Here is how one poet described Viking warships and warriors: "Full they were of fighters and flashing shields, war-lances and wound-blades…Men had hopes of bloodshed, howled like wolves, and brandished their weapons…"

20

TREASURE CHEST

One of the reasons for the Viking raids was to gain wealth. The original of this chest (this is a copy) was made from wood, gilt bronze, and elk antler. It probably contained some of the loot raided by the Vikings.

▲ Ready to attack
This carved stone, found at Lindisfarne, depicts Viking warriors armed with swords and battle-axes.

Viking violence

What was the reason for this Viking violence? Mostly the hope of snatching valuable loot. Churches, monasteries, and coastal towns all offered rich pickings for anyone who attacked. The Vikings took gold and silver crosses, silken embroideries and decorated books, along with cloth, jewels, and weapons. Young men, women, and children were carried off, to be sold as slaves. Older people were sometimes killed.

Like most other peoples, the Vikings went to war for two main reasons: to protect their homes and to

◀ King and martyr
A nineteenth century stained-glass window, showing Vikings killing King Edmund of East Anglia in AD 870. Edmund was a Christian, who refused to give up his faith. He was later made a saint.

conquer new lands. War was risky; the fate of an entire kingdom might be decided in a single battle. Bravery, strength, and skill were highly prized. Viking myths taught that "Odin's (god of battle and death) sons are those who die in battle." Men who were killed fighting would be rewarded after death.

Weapons and armor

Viking law-codes tell us that all adult men were meant to be trained and equipped for war. Farm work and sports like wrestling probably kept most men fit. Soldiers had to provide their own weapons and armor. These included a sword, shield, spear, and helmet; other men fought with axes, clubs, and catapults. Viking kings also paid workers from the towns, who had no land, to fight for them, so permanent royal armies were maintained.

Wealthy Vikings spent large sums of money on weapons that not only looked beautiful, but

DEFENSIVE WEAPONS

Viking soldiers carried shields to defend themselves, as well as weapons like swords and spears that were designed for attack. Viking shields were made of planks of wood, held together with strong iron nails. They were sometimes painted with elaborate designs. There was a large *boss*—a dome-shaped piece of iron—at the center of most shields. The warrior held the shield by a grip behind the boss, keeping it close to his arm. The boss protected his hand.

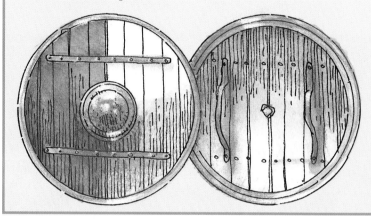

◄ **Wild horsemen**
This thirteenth-century Norwegian tapestry depicts a warrior on horseback. We know that the Vikings sometimes used horses in battle. They also rode them to go hunting and to make long journeys overland.

► **Fully armed**
This carving from a stone cross at Weston, North Yorkshire, shows a Viking warrior wielding a sword and a battle-ax. Although Vikings were skilled metalworkers, they believed that the best sword blades were made by the Franks (from northern France). They imported many high-priced weapons from Frankish lands.

worked well. Favorite swords might be passed on from father to son. Their blades were decorated with magical patterns, and they had names such as "fire of battle," "leg-biter," or "long and sharp." Rich Vikings also fought on horseback; this made them more mobile, more terrifying, and more difficult to attack.

"The rush of battle . . ."

Battle tactics were simple. The Vikings aimed to overpower their enemies by the force of their attack. The tenth-century Anglo-Saxon poem, *The Battle of Maldon*, describes the Viking impact, "They let the spears, hard as files, fly from their hands . . . . Bows were busy. Point pierced shield. The rush of battle was fierce, warriors fell on both sides, men lay dead." After a battle, the weapons, jewelry, and armor belonging to dead enemies were collected together and shared among the winning side.

◀ Precious weapons
Three swords, found at Viking sites in Denmark. Left: iron sword, decorated with brass. Center: iron sword, decorated with silver and brass. Right: iron sword with silver decorations on the hilt.

▶ Portrait of a Viking
This carved head, of elk horn, formed the handle of a stick. It shows a Swedish Viking, wearing a metal helmet with a guard-piece covering his nose. He has neatly trimmed hair and a short beard. Monks complained that Viking warriors lured British women away from British men, because the Vikings were clean and well dressed.

KINGS AND KINGDOMS

"A king is for glory, not for long life," King Magnus Barefoot of Norway (who died at about age thirty in AD 1103) was reported to have said. Viking poetry portrays kings as noble, daring, and brave. But what else did Viking kings do? How did they govern without a civil service, modern communications, or even nationally agreed upon laws?

Kings had to protect "the honor, safety, and well-being" of their people. Some were warriors; others were admired for promoting trade, or defending their kingdoms from attack. Kings needed the support of local lords and, toward the end of the Viking period, the help of royal officials as well. They relied on these men to protect law and order, to help collect taxes, and to give advice and leadership in war. Kings also traveled around, making friends with powerful men.

In Viking times, a king's oldest son did not always inherit his father's crown. Each new king had to prove his fitness for the task, through political intrigue (perhaps helped by his mother and her family), by winning the approval of the

▶ **In the high seat**
Large Viking halls were furnished with benches around the side, plus a *high seat*, framed with carved pillars, where the most important man sat. Kings used high seats as their thrones.

▶ **Remembering a king**
Copy of a memorial stone made for King Harald Bluetooth of Denmark, who died in 987. The original stone still survives at the Danish royal burial ground, Jelling.

▼ **Daring deeds**
This whalebone box was made around 700 in the north of England, shortly before the Vikings attacked. Its panels portray the myths and legends of many lands. In this scene, Egil, a great archer, is defending his house against the enemy.

people he governed and, sometimes, by fighting to seize the throne.

Powerful women

Viking women did not become rulers, but they played an important role in other ways. The daughters or widows of great men were eagerly sought in marriage, for political reasons. In 1017 King Cnut married Queen Emma, the widow of the English King Æthelred, because he thought it would make the English people more willing to accept him as their king.

KINGS AND COINS

Viking kings issued coins when they came to power. An iron die (see below) was made to form coins by stamping silver. The die was struck with a hammer onto a silver blank, which had already been cut and weighed. Also shown in the picture is a lead trial-piece, which was used to test the die.

▲ Some coins bore a portrait of the king, or carried a symbol which the Vikings recognized as belonging to their leader. This penny with a bird symbol was made for Anlaf Guthfrisson, King at York from 939–941.

VIKING PEOPLE

Viking people were not all equal. Some were rich, some poor. Some owned vast estates, others made do with a simple cottage. A few had dozens of slaves to work for them, other families did most tasks for themselves. Some Vikings were not even free; instead, they belonged to wealthier people and could not run away. People from other countries also lived in the Viking lands—there were traders, missionary priests, captives, and hostages, as well as slaves who were bought on expeditions.

A Viking legend tells the story of how their society began. The story is not true, but the poem reveals that the Vikings originally thought of themselves as belonging to one of three groups. These were *jarls* (lords), *bondi* (farmers), and *thralls* (servants, who were treated almost like slaves).

According to the legend, each group had different responsibilities, and lived in a different

▼ Proud families
Memorial stone from Uppland, Sweden, carved with runes and a cross. These memorials showed that Vikings remembered dead relations with love and respect.

▲ Lucky charm?
Portraits of Viking people are rare. This little figure of a Viking woman was made of gilt bronze, and was possibly worn as a charm or an ornament.

RUNES

The Vikings used a form of writing called runes. The letters were spiky, because they were the easiest shapes to carve on wood.

At first the alphabet had 24 runes; later, only 16. Below: the shorter runic alphabet, known as the *futhark* after its first six letters.

f u th a r k h n

i a s t b m l R

way. Jarls owned land; this made them rich. They were also war leaders, brave fighters, and generous. Their wives were beautiful and gracious, their sons strong, handsome, well educated, and wise. They had names like Noble, Heir, or King. Bondi worked on the land; they were tough, eager, hardworking, and knew all about land and livestock. Their wives were busy, capable housekeepers. Their children were called Blacksmith, Settler, Weaver, and Quick. Thralls had a miserable time. They did hard, dirty work, ate poor food, and wore ragged clothes. Their children's names tell us more about their lives: boys were called Cattleman, Foolish, and Grumpy; girls were named Torn-Skirt, Quarreler, and Clumsy.

This legend exaggerates and simplifies so as to entertain. But it paints a recognizable picture of Viking society, even though there were other important Viking people, like merchants, fishermen, craftsmen, teachers, and poets.

▲ **Precious people**
Two more figures showing Viking people, this time made of silver. The man, found in a tenth-century grave at Birka in Sweden, rides jauntily on horseback. The woman, from Öland in Sweden, holds out a welcoming drinking horn. In real life, this would have been filled with *mead*, a sweet alcoholic drink made from honey. She wears her hair tied back in a loose knot, and wears a flowing robe with a train.

SOCIAL STRUCTURE

Kings and lords were the leaders of Viking society. They were powerful because they were war leaders, wealthy and wise—or, at least, cunning.

Farmers formed the backbone of society. They, too, could be rich and powerful, if they owned livestock and good farming land.

Thralls were at the bottom of society. They were poor and not free. Laws protected them from being treated harshly.

Slaves were not full members of society. They were possessions, like horses or cattle. But if they worked hard and pleased their owners, slaves could be set free.

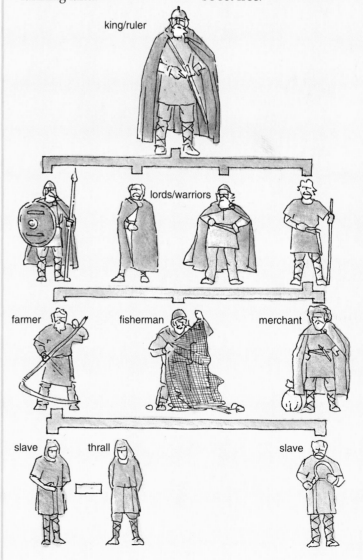

king/ruler

lords/warriors

farmer   fisherman   merchant

slave   thrall   slave

COMMUNITY LIFE

Viking government was based in local communities. There were good reasons for this. The Scandinavian landscape is rough and rugged; even short journeys could take several days. If there were thefts and murders or other serious crimes, or simply quarrels between neighbors, you could not always wait for the king's officials to arrive. You needed a quick, local way of restoring law and order.

Life-styles varied widely in different Viking regions, so local laws had to be made to suit local conditions. For example, local villagers had to agree how to sort out disputes over fishing rights, or over new lands shared by settlers in Iceland and Greenland.

Things

The Vikings held village meetings, called "Things," to make local laws and investigate crimes. Things met twice a year, and all free adult men were expected to attend. Here taxes were arranged, weapons checked, and serious crimes investigated. In the early Viking age, Things also helped to choose a new king. Meetings were controlled by a *law-speaker*. He asked everyone to vote on decisions by rattling their weapons together—this noisy signal was called a *vápnatak*. The Vikings obeyed these democratic decisions—on the whole—for the good of the community.

Serious crimes

Things lasted for almost a week. One day was set aside for trials of serious crimes. The suspected criminal, and the people who accused him (or her), stood before the law-speaker and a group of well-respected men. Both sides brought witnesses to prove that what they said was true. The more witnesses they could produce, the more they were believed. If witnesses could not be found, the suspect might be tested by an ordeal, or (for men only) by fighting a duel. Punishments could be severe. Criminals were fined, stoned, outlawed, and sometimes killed.

FROM A MERCHANT'S PACK

These three folding scales were found at the busy Viking trading city of York, together with a set of lead weights. Folding scales were made for traveling merchants. Scales like these were used to weigh small, precious objects.

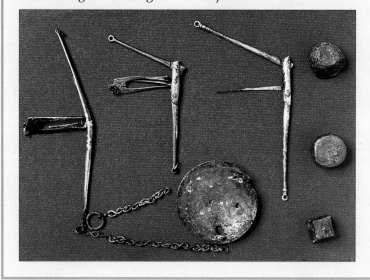

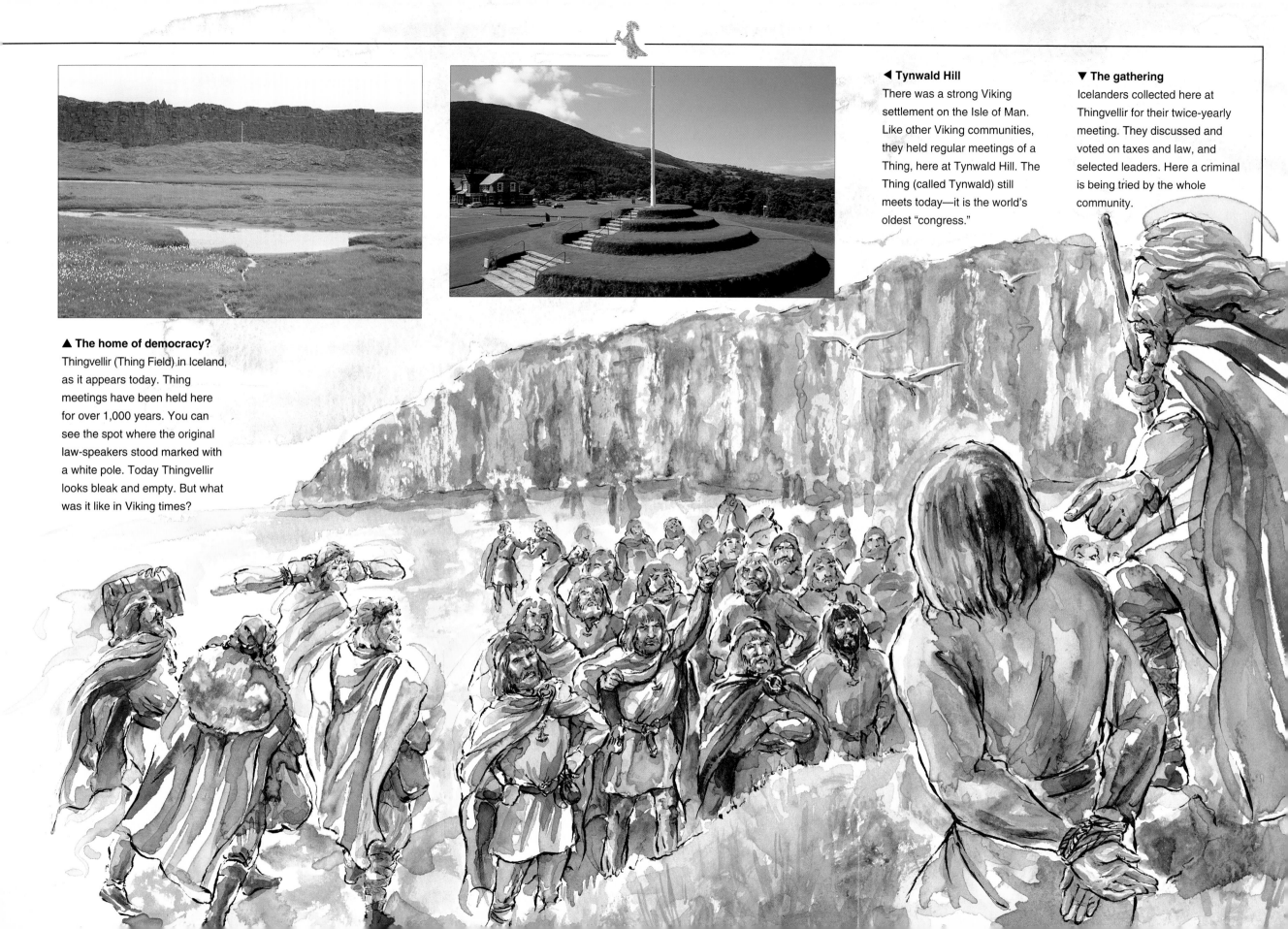

◄ Tynwald Hill

There was a strong Viking settlement on the Isle of Man. Like other Viking communities, they held regular meetings of a Thing, here at Tynwald Hill. The Thing (called Tynwald) still meets today—it is the world's oldest "congress."

▼ The gathering

Icelanders collected here at Thingvellir for their twice-yearly meeting. They discussed and voted on taxes and law, and selected leaders. Here a criminal is being tried by the whole community.

▲ The home of democracy?

Thingvellir (Thing Field) in Iceland, as it appears today. Thing meetings have been held here for over 1,000 years. You can see the spot where the original law-speakers stood marked with a white pole. Today Thingvellir looks bleak and empty. But what was it like in Viking times?

▼ **A busy marketplace?**
This bleak landscape in Iceland was a very important place for the whole island. Twice a year the whole area slowly drew people to it. Here the market people are setting up their stalls and spreading out their wares in the hope that others will venture to this isolated spot. Why should merchants expect a gathering?

FOOD AND FARMING

T he environment in which the Vikings lived was harsh. For many people, their most important task was growing enough food to eat. In cold, wet summers, when harvests failed, shortages and starvation were a real danger. Some historians think this is why so many Vikings left their homelands to settle in warmer, more plentiful lands.

▼ **A food factory**
Farmhouses like this, in Iceland, were centers of essential food production. Without the skills of Viking farmers, their wives, and their servants, Viking people would go hungry, or starve.

Today, the Scandinavian climate is cold. The weather was slightly warmer in Viking times, but snow fell from October to February, and the land was frozen hard. In the far north, beyond the Arctic Circle, winter temperatures fell to around 20°F (–7°C). Summers could be warm and sunny but, compared with most of Europe, they were short. There was only a little time for food crops to grow.

Porridge and stew
Some fields in Denmark, southern Norway, and Sweden were fertile and easily plowed.

HUNTING FOR FOOD

Although some Viking farmers reared domestic animals for food, this did not happen in all areas. So wild animals like these were hunted as an alternative source of meat. They were useful for other products too. Furs became valuable warm clothing and were one of the chief exports. Bone and antler were used for knife handles and combs.

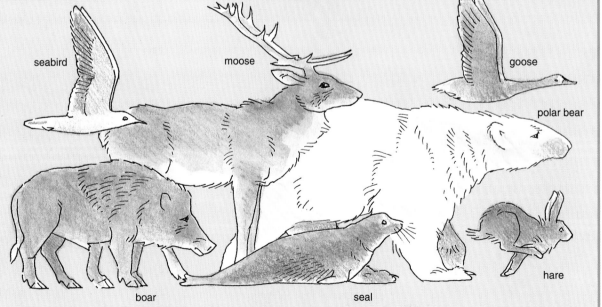

seabird

moose

goose

polar bear

boar

seal

hare

FOR FOOD AND FIREWOOD

Snow and ice covered the Viking lands for many months each year. Carts were useless in deep snow, so the Vikings made sleds to pull heavy loads of food or firewood over the frozen ground. This carved wooden sled comes from the Oseberg royal ship-burial. Not all Viking sleds would have been as well made or finely decorated.

Elsewhere, the land was stony and poor. Viking farmers grew barley, oats, and rye, which the women ground by hand and cooked to make heavy porridge or bread. When food was scarce, they mixed flour with acorns or pine bark. It must have tasted dry and very bitter. Farmers also grew vegetables—peas, beans, cabbage, turnips, onions, and garlic. Cows, horses, sheep, and goats provided milk and meat; pigs, chickens, and geese were reared. When they could afford it, Viking families enjoyed soups and stews.

Winter supplies

Viking farmers and their wives had to know how to preserve enough food to last through the long, cold winters. There were no food shops, except in the towns. If a family's stock of grain became damp and moldy, or was eaten by mice, then everyone would go hungry. Meat was pickled and smoked. Butter and cheese were kept in cold, airy storerooms. Peas, beans, and onions were carefully dried. Some historians think that the Vikings also used the winter snow as an early form of deep freeze.

Vikings could not have survived by farming alone. They made good use of the natural resources that surrounded their fields and farms.

FARMING TOOLS

For plowing and harvesting, tools like those below were used. The ard was a simple plow. It broke up the earth with the downward directed point and was pulled along by a couple of animals held on the harness. Vikings also used a more sophisticated plow that turned the earth with a plowshare. Scythes and sickles were used for harvesting crops. They were normally made from iron with wooden handles.

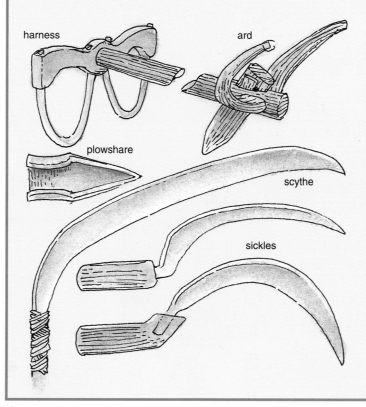

harness

ard

plowshare

scythe

sickles

Forests and moorland provided wild foods of many kinds.

Archaeologists have found seeds and stones from cherries, plums, blackberries, raspberries, strawberries, blueberries, elderberries, and sloes at many Viking sites. Nuts, acorns, and mushrooms were collected by women and children, and stored

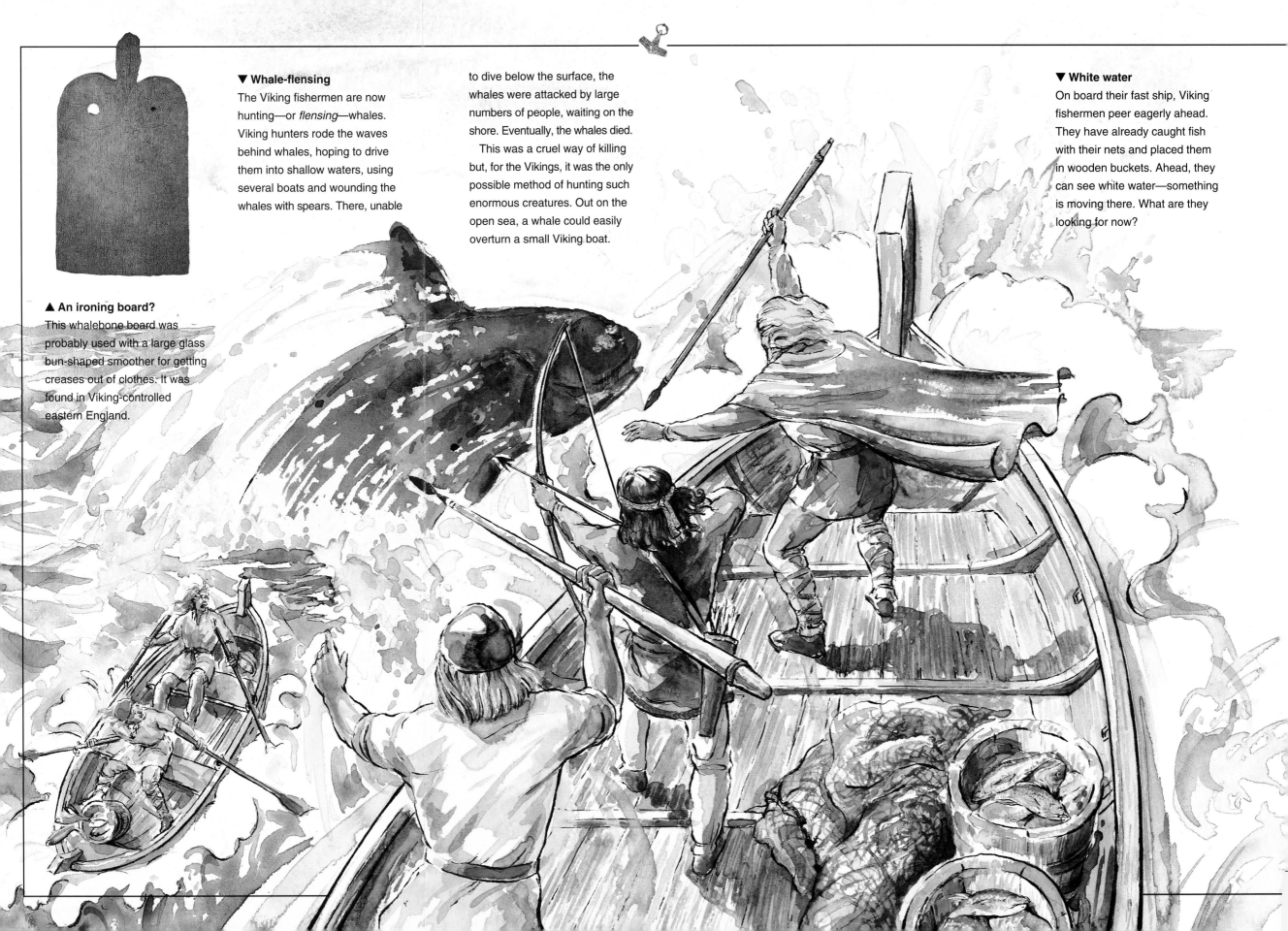

▼ Whale-flensing

The Viking fishermen are now hunting—or *flensing*—whales. Viking hunters rode the waves behind whales, hoping to drive them into shallow waters, using several boats and wounding the whales with spears. There, unable to dive below the surface, the whales were attacked by large numbers of people, waiting on the shore. Eventually, the whales died.

This was a cruel way of killing but, for the Vikings, it was the only possible method of hunting such enormous creatures. Out on the open sea, a whale could easily overturn a small Viking boat.

▲ An ironing board?

This whalebone board was probably used with a large glass bun-shaped smoother for getting creases out of clothes. It was found in Viking-controlled eastern England.

▼ White water

On board their fast ship, Viking fishermen peer eagerly ahead. They have already caught fish with their nets and placed them in wooden buckets. Ahead, they can see white water—something is moving there. What are they looking for now?

for winter use. Honey and herbs were gathered to make drinks, medicines, and lucky charms. Along the coast, seaweed was pulled from the rocks. It was cooked and eaten as a vegetable, or boiled up with water to provide valuable salt.

Food from the sea

The Viking lands were surrounded by oceans, and the Vikings were great sailors. So it is not surprising that they searched for food from the sea. The Vikings went fishing for cod and herrings, which they ate fresh, or preserved by salting or drying in the wind. Dried cod was eaten with butter and coarse rye bread. Rock pools along the seashores provided shellfish of various kinds, and steep cliffs sheltered seabirds like puffins and gulls. The Vikings raided their nests for eggs and hunted them to eat. The Vikings also experimented with fish-farming in freshwater lakes.

Food, feathers, and fur

Many wild creatures were also hunted and killed. They provided food, and also skins, fur, and bones. Rabbits and hares, along with ducks, geese, and other wild birds, were shot or trapped in nets. As well as providing welcome meat, the birds' feathers were used to make warm mattresses and quilts.

Bears, foxes, and squirrels were shot with bows and arrows for their thick, warm fur. Deer—including reindeer—were highly prized. Their antlers were used to make knife handles, their bones were sawed and polished for combs, and their skins were cut into strips to use as ropes.

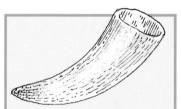

▲ Delicate decoration
Bone is a smooth material that can be delicately carved. Viking craftworkers used it to make fine objects like this end-piece for a leather belt or strap.

DRINK AND BE MERRY?

Eyewitnesses reported that the Vikings were very fond of alcoholic drinks. Wealthy people drank wine, but most people drank beer made from barley and hops, or mead, a strong, sweet drink made from honey.

Drinking was part of social life—no feast was complete without it—and also part of some religious ceremonies. Drinks were served in the hollowed-out horns of sheep and oxen, or else in horn-shaped beakers made of glass.

Drunkenness was common. Critics of the Vikings claimed that some Viking men died from the effects of too much drink.

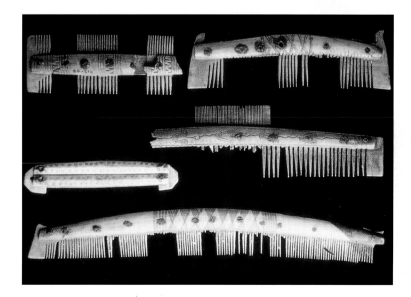

◀ Fine-tooth combs
Bone could be cut and polished to make combs, like these, found at York. Wealthy men and women purchased combs elaborately carved with pictures and patterns. These combs were used to tidy the hair and to comb out unwanted parasites, such as fleas and lice. Keeping clean for special occasions was important. One Viking poet advised: "Each man should set off for the Thing freshly washed and well filled with food."

HOUSES AND HOMES

"Better a house of your own, however small it might be. Everybody is somebody at home. Two goats and a badly roofed cottage are better than begging," claimed one Viking poet. Many Viking men and women lived in small, simple houses which, at times, they could not even afford to repair.

At the beginning of the Viking age, most people worked in the countryside, but by AD 1000, an increasing number were living in towns. The most important early towns were Hedeby (in Denmark), Helgö and Birka (in Sweden), and Kaupang (in Norway). They all began to decay by the eleventh century and were overtaken by new towns set up by Viking kings.

▼ Hall-houses

The remains of a ninth-century Viking dwelling at Birsay, in Orkney. This large dwelling had one room, 65 feet (20 m) in length. Animals were kept in separate buildings.

Town life

Town life was not always pleasant. At Hedeby,

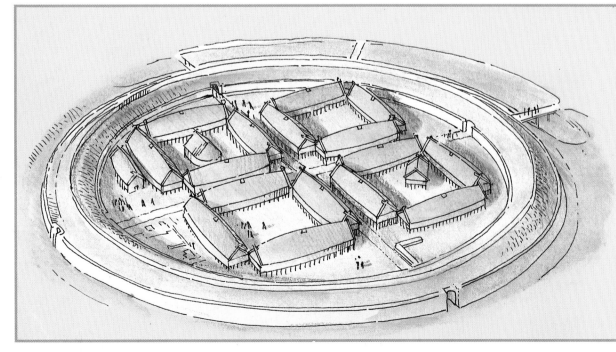

A VIKING FORT

This settlement is a reconstruction of a tenth-century Viking fort at Fyrkat in Denmark. Forts like this were centers of royal power, providing living quarters for soldiers, women, and children. A mound of earth, topped by a fence and surrounded by a ditch, provided protection for the buildings.

poor families lived in thatched huts made of wattle and daub that occupied 35 square feet (3m²). These were built with a sunken earth floor and a fireplace in one corner. Conditions inside must have been dark, smoky, and unhealthily damp. It is perhaps no surprise to discover, from the evidence of burials, that ordinary Hedeby citizens could not expect to live more than 40 years. Houses in Hedeby did not last even that long. When a hut began to rot, it was simply pulled down, and a new building put up in its place.

In contrast, wealthy people in Hedeby lived in comfortable, well-built homes. The town's main streets were carefully planned and "paved" with wooden planks to keep them free of mud. Fresh water came from wells or from a stream; rubbish was disposed of in cesspits and sewers.

Archaeologists have excavated several houses, owned by craftsmen and merchants. Each is about 50 feet (15 m) long and 20 feet (6 m) wide. They are surrounded by gardens, workshops, and stores. The town itself, which covered 60 acres, was defended with a high earth bank, topped with a fence.

Family life

"Be patient with your kinsfolk," said one Viking poet. This was good advice. Vikings depended on their families for food, shelter, companionship, protection—and revenge. It was good to know that there was one group of people you could always rely on, who would fight on your side and punish anyone who attacked you. Feuds were common, starting if someone felt a family member had been

▼ Stone and turf
In Iceland, Orkney, and Shetland, stone and turf was used for building. Trees did not grow, so wood had to be imported, and was expensive. Straw was used to make dry beds for animals kept indoors during the long winter months; it could not be spared for roofing.

POTTERY AND STONE

This pottery vessel is a Torksey-ware pot, found in York, from the Viking period. It may not have been made by Vikings. Although they were skillful craftworkers, pottery was a craft they ignored—most of their bowls were made of soapstone. Viking pottery was crude, simple, and rare. Elsewhere in Europe potters were making beautiful bowls and dishes, using clever techniques.

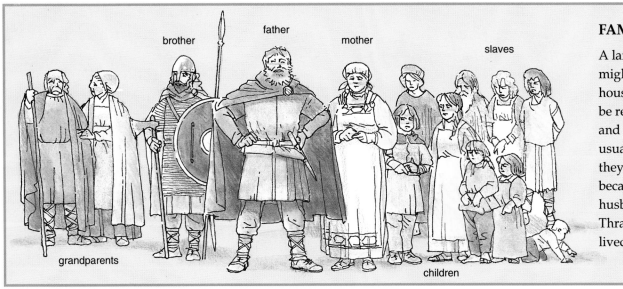

father

brother

mother

slaves

grandparents

children

FAMILY GROUP

A large number of people might live in one Viking household. Many would be related—sons, brothers, and cousins. Women usually left home when they were married, and became part of their husband's family group. Thralls and slaves also lived and worked here.

insulted. The head of a family—the oldest man—might even say prayers and make offerings to the gods on behalf of the family as a whole.

By *kinsfolk*, the Vikings meant a much larger group than most people think of as their family today. For example, in Jutland (part of Denmark) "kin" included everyone descended from the same great-great-grandparents. Family groups living together were also larger than is usual nowadays. In the early Viking age, all the young men of one family, their wives, and children might live with parents and grandparents, and work together on the family farm.

Shared responsibility

At home, everyone had important jobs to do. Men worked in the fields, went hunting, and looked after livestock. Women cooked, cared for children, spun and wove wool, sewed, embroidered, washed clothes, worked in the dairy making butter and cheese, concocted medicines (and sometimes spells), and cared for the sick. They supervised male and female slaves, and knew how to run the farm

▶ **Kitchen tools**
If Viking poets are to be believed, Viking housewives and servants were good cooks. But they used simple utensils. Their spoons were made of wood or bone, or iron with a tin coating.

while their sons and husbands were away. In wartime, or in fishing villages, this could be for months or years at a time.

Sons and daughters were trained by their parents, although, once the Vikings became Christians, a few boys and girls were educated in church schools. Daughters usually left home when they married to join their husband's family. Some men—we do not know how many—left their farms for a while, to go on Viking raids.

IN THE KITCHEN

Cooking equipment like this has been found in Viking houses and farms. Bowls and dishes of pottery or soapstone were used for storing, serving, or cooking food. A gridiron was used for holding meat over flames to grill it. Metal pans were also used for cooking vegetables and soups.

wooden bucket

pottery cooking pots

gridiron

iron knife

wooden cup

▶ Viking meals

At ordinary meals, the Vikings ate simply. Bread, soup, fish, meat, and cheese were the main items in their diet. On feast days, they ate more. But even if their food was simple, the Vikings loved to entertain. The tenth-century German writer, Adam of Bremen, commented that the Swedish people, in particular, had a strong tradition of hospitality. Guests were made very welcome, with good food, strong drink, and a warm bed.

ENTERTAINMENT

In summer, there was always work to do. But Vikings took time off, to go swimming, to have picnics, to watch wrestling matches, or to arrange (cruel) fights between animals, especially stallions. But winters were cold, and the dark nights were very long. In the far north, daylight lasted for only three or four hours. Snow lay all around and it was impossible to work in the fields. How did the Vikings pass the time?

For women, work continued much as before, perhaps with the extra problem of drying wet, snowy clothes. Men and boys repaired buildings and tools, and practiced their fighting skills. Sleds, skis, and skates made of horses' shin bones were used for journeys, and also for fun. There were indoor amusements like *merils*, a form of

▼ **Kings, queens, and bishops**
Chess pieces found on the island of Lewis, off Scotland, carved from walrus ivory. Chess was known in Iceland by the twelfth century, and may have been played in the Viking homelands before then.

▲ **Wine from the Rhine**
This pottery wine jug was found at Birka in Sweden. The climate of Scandinavia was too cold for grapes to grow, yet rich Vikings enjoyed wine. So they imported it from Germany and France.

checkers. The Vikings were also great gamblers. Yule (January 12 by our modern calendar), which marked the turning point of winter, was celebrated by a splendid feast.

Feasting all year-round

The Vikings enjoyed feasting at any time of the year. Rich men invited their friends to a feast on special occasions, like the end of harvest or the return from a successful raid. Feasts also displayed a lord's wealth and power. A war-leader rewarded his soldiers with a generous meal and vast quantities of drink. These celebrations could last for several days; people ate too much, got drunk, quarreled, sang, and laughed. Sometimes there were fights. Thoughtful hosts stationed lookouts at the doors, to make sure that enemies did not attack while they were too full of food to fight.

▲ Board games
Hnefatafl was a board game in which a "king" had to be protected by his men against attackers. The board is a modern copy, but the dark counters are Viking originals.

▼ Lucky chance
The Vikings liked to gamble and make bets. These dice, of walrus ivory, and drilled with holes to mark the spots, are typical of many found in Viking towns.

WINTER SPORTS

There was snow and ice in the Viking lands for several months each year. This made journeys difficult. But some people used skates and sleds to travel—or race for fun— across frozen rivers and lakes. The Vikings also had snowshoes and skis. This leather boot with a skate of polished bone was found in Viking York.

▲ Musical tunes
The Vikings were also fond of music. Victories were celebrated in songs, and dead comrades were mourned with poems. Both might be accompanied on the harp or lyre. Some Viking musical instruments, like these bone pipes, have been found at Viking sites.

VIKING CRAFTS

Everything the Vikings used—from battleaxes to the finest silken cloth—was made by hand. There were no big machines, so craftworkers were essential to the Viking way of life. Without them, the Vikings could not have farmed, fought, cooked, gone on journeys, housed, or clothed themselves.

Viking farmers and laborers could do simple woodwork, and repair iron tools. Viking women and girls spent many hours each day spinning thread and weaving cloth. Blacksmiths, builders, and makers of rough furniture could be found in most villages. But for everything else they needed, the Vikings traveled to the towns, where craftsmen (and a few craftswomen) had their workshops and sold their goods.

▼ **Golden horns**
Some Viking drinking horns were made of real ox horn, hollowed and polished; others were made of metal. These are replicas of horns made shortly before the Viking era.

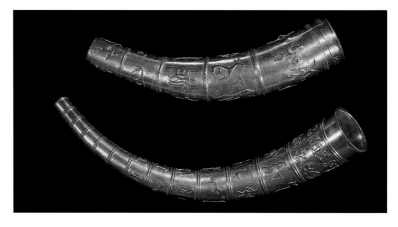

▲ **The glitter of gold**
This tenth-century gold brooch was found in Hornelund in Denmark. Gold filigree wire and gold granules have been soldered onto a gold sheet backplate. Viking goldsmiths made elaborate and finely worked jewelry.

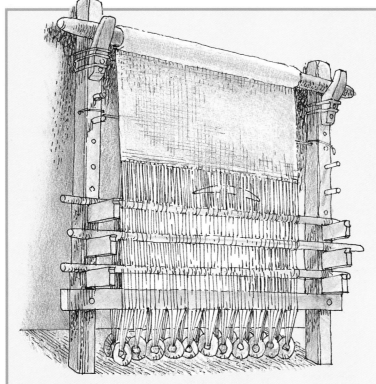

WOMEN'S WORK

A large wooden loom stood in the corner of many Viking rooms. This was where the women of the household wove cloth from wool and flax to make clothes for family members. They used fleece from their own sheep; they spun the fleece themselves. When the wool was woven into cloth they would also dye it. In towns, you could buy cloth, but it was very expensive.

BRILLIANT GLASS BEADS

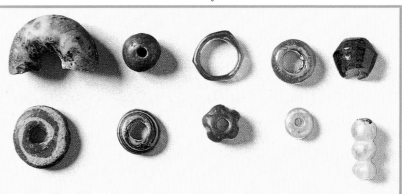

The Vikings did not make glass themselves, but they were skillful glassworkers, all the same. They imported sticks of colored glass from craft workers in Italy and Germany, heated them, and fused them into complicated patterns. Then they shaped them into beads, which were strung together to make brightly colored necklaces. These beads were found in York.

Well-made goods

From discoveries at Viking sites, we know that visitors to Viking workshops might buy carved wooden dishes, soapstone bowls, or iron pots for cooking. Loom weights, made of pottery or stone, were another essential purchase. Cheap bronze brooches and hairpins (which were easily lost, and needed replacing) fastened cloaks and kerchiefs. Wealthy customers chose massive brooches made of gold and silver, and strings of jet, glass, or amber beads.

Viking merchants returning from a profitable trading trip, or young men sailing home from Viking raids, might also come to the towns, to exchange some of their treasures for armor, clothes, and weapons for themselves, or trappings for their horses. Leather bridles, decorated with silver, have been found in Viking graves, along with carved wooden horse collars and a magnificent wooden chariot. From the evidence of all these finds, it is clear that Viking craftworkers were very highly skilled.

▼ **Hammering metal**
The blacksmith was a key member of the Viking village community. He made and mended weapons, tools, and farm equipment, forged chains and anchors, and mass-produced nails used in building ships and houses.

CLOTHES AND JEWELRY

Viking men and women took great pride in their appearance. According to the tenth-century Arab traveler Ibn Fadlan, this was perfectly understandable. "Never have I seen people of more perfect physique," he wrote, "they are as tall as date-palms, and reddish in color." Another Arab geographer, Ibn Rustah, also described them as "well built and good-looking."

Warm clothes were essential, but Viking men and women also spent money on fine fabrics, rich embroideries, and impressive jewels. Tapestries and carvings show that a Viking woman wore a long linen shift with a sleeveless woolen dress on top. If she was wealthy (and did not have to do dirty work) the dress might be embroidered or edged with braid. It might also have a train. She wrapped herself in a flowing cloak, which she could let slip from her shoulders to reveal white, graceful arms— or so the poets said. Her hair grew long, and she

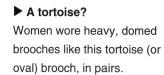
► A tortoise?
Women wore heavy, domed brooches like this tortoise (or oval) brooch, in pairs.

▲ From Viking York
Viking men and women wore rings on their fingers, and also arm rings, rather like bracelets. These were often given by lords to reward brave, faithful warriors after a battle or raid. This silver finger ring was made in the late ninth or early tenth century, and was found in the Viking city of York.

▲ Equipped for the next world
Viking men and women were often buried with their favorite possessions—helmets and spears for men, combs and jewelry for women. This tells us that the Vikings believed in some form of life after death. This is part of a bridle mount that was buried with a man in Broa on Gotland.

BOOTS AND SHOES

Vikings wore leather shoes, with woolen socks to keep their feet warm. Archaeologists have unearthed many Viking boots and shoes at York, along with a leatherworker's stall, dated AD 948. This photo shows a modern reconstruction of a Viking shoe, based on the discoveries at York.

▶ **Gilt bronze cloak pin**
Viking winter clothes were thick and heavy, to keep out the cold. They were fastened with ring-brooches like this, from Denmark.

▲ **A rich display**
A Viking woman's wealth was measured by the jewelry she wore. Necklaces and brooches were favorites. Ordinary women could not afford real gold jewelry, so they chose ornate pieces like these delicate earrings found in Sweden.

fastened it into a loose knot at the back of her head. Usually she wore a kerchief, several large brooches, and strings of beads. She kept her feet warm with woolen stockings and leather boots or shoes.

Makeup for men?

Viking men wore thick woolen tunics, belted at the waist, over long leggings or baggy trousers. Like the women, they wore warm cloaks, socks, and boots. They had caps made from leather, fur, or expensive imported silk. Viking men liked jewelry—gold and silver bracelets, necklaces, and rings were given by kings to reward men who fought bravely in battle. Ibn Fadlan, in his report quoted on page 42, also claimed that Viking men and women wore eye makeup, "so that their beauty never fades."

VIKING GODS AND MYTHS

Almost all past societies believed in one or several gods. The Vikings had a large number but did not worship them all equally. People might choose one god as a special protector, or they might pray to different gods to suit their different needs.

The Vikings worshiped two different families of gods. The most ancient group, known as the Vanir, controlled fertility, peace, and plenty. People in Scandinavia had prayed to them for thousands of years. The most important members of this family were Frey (which means lord) and his sister Freya (which means lady). They gave generous harvests, watched over the birth of children and animals, and helped everything to grow. Their statues were carried around the countryside on carts, bringing good luck and an end to war.

▶ **God of plenty**
Little bronze statue of the god Frey, perhaps purchased by a farmer to protect his crops and livestock, or by a woman, to help her bear healthy children.

◀ **A god's protection**
A silver pendant, made to hang from a chain or thong worn around the neck. It probably shows the face of a god.

▶ **Christian and pagan**
This carving is from a stone cross at Kirk Andreas (St. Andreas Church) on the Isle of Man. It shows scenes from Viking legends about the gods. Here, Odin (with a raven and a spear) is being attacked by a monster called the Fenris-Wolf at Ragnarok—the end of the world.

The Aesir

The newer family of gods was known as the Aesir. They stood for values that were prized in Viking society. The Aesir family contained many members—some more likable than others. The two most important Aesir gods were Odin and Thor. Odin was the god of battle. He gave victory to his followers, but sometimes they paid a high price. This was because Odin was also the god of madness, confusion, and fury. Odin was unpredictable and untrustworthy, but he was also very clever. He tortured himself so that he could understand runes. He wrote wonderful poetry. He was a magician who could change his shape. He could talk to the birds, and see into the future.

Thor was a much simpler character. He was also more popular; many Viking men wore a good luck charm (shaped like the hammer Thor always carried) on a leather thong around their neck. Thor was the god of storms, thunder, strength, and hard work. It was thought that he rode a chariot across the sky, which created storms. He protected ordinary men and women in their daily lives. In

▲ **A sign from the gods?**
A poor animal met its death, hanged as a sacrifice to the gods. Worshipers perhaps hoped to hear the rumbling of Thor's chariot (a crash of thunder) and Thor's mighty hammer hurtling down from the sky (lightning), as a sign that he had accepted the sacrifice. The Vikings believed that thunderstorms revealed Thor's terrifying strength and majesty.

To please the gods, the Vikings sacrificed weapons and animals (and occasionally people) in this way.

THOR'S HAMMER
Amulets like this silver hammer from Denmark have been found at many Viking sites. Wearers hoped Thor would protect them. Silver hammers were also attractive jewelry. Viking craftsmen made them in several different designs; in the later Viking period, when missionaries were spreading Christianity, they also made crosses for people to wear.

▼ Outside the temple

At Uppsala, in Sweden, there was a temple containing three great images of the gods Odin, Thor, and Frey. People came from miles around to offer prayers to each of these gods—to all-powerful Thor when sickness and hunger threatened, to furious Odin in wartime, and to peaceful Frey when marriages were being celebrated.

Priests led the worshipers away from the temple building, toward a huge evergreen tree in the middle of a sacred wood (below). It was said that no one knew how old the tree was, or what species it was. But it never lost its leaves, and looked fresh and flourishing throughout the year. A holy spring ran through the wood and everything was dedicated to the gods. The priests took care to keep unbelievers at a distance, for fear that they would pollute this special holy place. It was at this tree that…

many ways, he was just like them, but better—a kind of super-hero.

Viking skalds entertained their audiences with poems and stories, which they recited from memory. Sometimes they included jokes about famous people and recent events. The Vikings liked quick thinking by poets, and other people, too.

Admiring stories were told about the warrior-poet Thormod. As he lay dying after a battle, he bravely pulled the arrow which had injured him from his wound. It was covered with blood and pieces of flesh. Thormod turned this into a grim joke about physical fitness. "You can tell the king feeds us well," he said, "Look, I have plenty of fat around my heart."

Monsters and magic

Thormod was a hero who actually existed. Other Viking stories were based on ancient myths and legends. Nobody knew or cared whether they were

▲ The story of Sigurd

Two adventures from the action-packed life of the Viking hero Sigurd, told in carvings on the wooden door posts from Hylestad Church in Setesdal, Norway. They were made around AD 1200, after the end of the Viking era, but record earlier Viking myths.
Left: Sigurd kills a dragon, using a magic sword made by Regin the Blacksmith. Sigurd wants the dragon's treasure.
Right: Sigurd kills Regin, who is plotting to seize the dragon's treasure for himself.

▶ A heavenly hoofprint?

A huge rock outcrop at Asbyrgi, Iceland, left by an ancient volcano. Local Viking legends told that the rocks heaved up like this when the hoof of the magic horse Sleipnir (see page 11) once touched the ground.

The horse Sleipnir belonged to the god Odin; in Viking carvings, it is sometimes shown galloping across the sky. Odin could talk to Sleipnir, and to his pet ravens—Thought and Memory—who flew alongside them on their mysterious, terrifying travels.

true, but they were fun. Some were about battles, others about love and romance. Some told tales of monsters, mystery, and magic. Many described the adventures of gods, goddesses, and kings.

The end of the world

Myths and legends also helped the Vikings think about their place in the world. One of the most important concerned the ending of our universe, a time the Vikings called Ragnarok. It predicted an era of cold and darkness, when brothers and sisters fought one another, and awful crimes took place. There was disease, disloyalty, and famine. Gods

battled with monsters, and the whole earth was swallowed up by the sea. But all was not lost. A new, peaceful, and even more beautiful world emerged from the darkness, and life began again.

Like all myths, this story dealt with topics that concern everyone. Viking life was a struggle against cold and hunger. They relied on families and comrades for support. There were many things they could not control, like storms, sickness, and the sea. The legend of Ragnarok showed what might happen when everything went wrong. But it also gave Viking people hope that things might get better in the future.

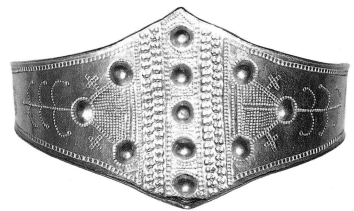

▲ Tree of life
Viking legends described Yggdrasil (the Tree of Life), which stretched from the heavens above to hell below, and whose branches covered the earth. Magic birds and animals perched among its leaves, and two wells, containing the water of wisdom and the water of destiny, were sheltered by its roots. It was always dying, yet always renewed. This powerful image of the environment was used to decorate clothes and jewels, like this tenth-century gold arm ring from Denmark.

▶ The end of the world
Heimdall was the watchman at the gates of heaven, where the gods lived. Their glorious home could only be approached across a fragile rainbow bridge. In this tenth-century stone carving from the Isle of Man, Heimdall is shown blowing his watchman's horn. This echoed around the world, and was an urgent summons for all the gods to gather together, because danger threatened. In some Viking myths, the sound of Heimdall's horn marked the beginning of Ragnarok—the end of the world.

▼ Farewell to the chief
It is a cold, wintry day in AD 922. The *Rus*—Viking adventurers who have settled in northern Russia—are busy in their camp. Their chief has just died, but there is drinking and feasting, music and songs. A huge fire is burning and a crowd has gathered around it. What is being burned?

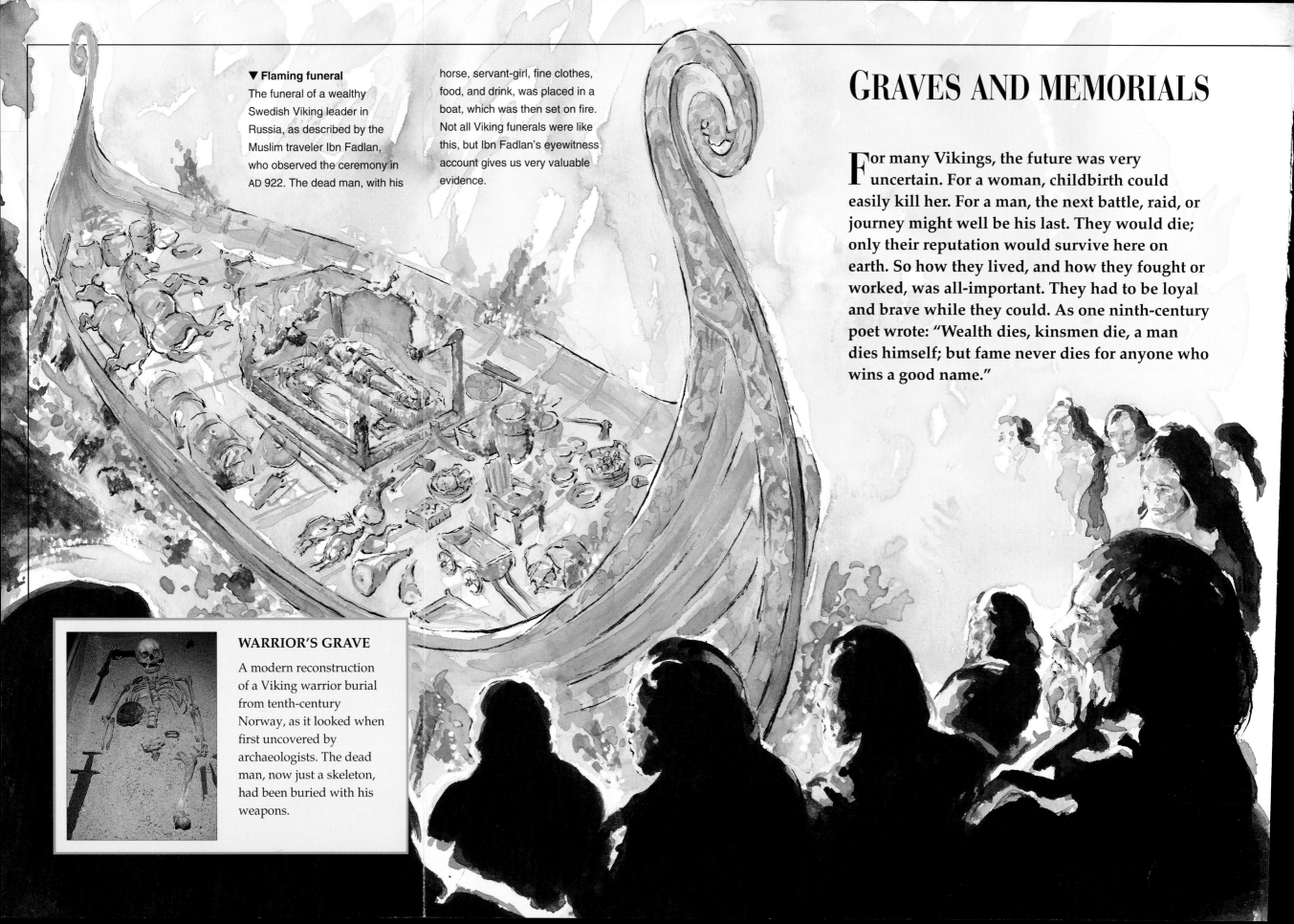

▼ Flaming funeral

The funeral of a wealthy Swedish Viking leader in Russia, as described by the Muslim traveler Ibn Fadlan, who observed the ceremony in AD 922. The dead man, with his horse, servant-girl, fine clothes, food, and drink, was placed in a boat, which was then set on fire. Not all Viking funerals were like this, but Ibn Fadlan's eyewitness account gives us very valuable evidence.

GRAVES AND MEMORIALS

For many Vikings, the future was very uncertain. For a woman, childbirth could easily kill her. For a man, the next battle, raid, or journey might well be his last. They would die; only their reputation would survive here on earth. So how they lived, and how they fought or worked, was all-important. They had to be loyal and brave while they could. As one ninth-century poet wrote: "Wealth dies, kinsmen die, a man dies himself; but fame never dies for anyone who wins a good name."

WARRIOR'S GRAVE

A modern reconstruction of a Viking warrior burial from tenth-century Norway, as it looked when first uncovered by archaeologists. The dead man, now just a skeleton, had been buried with his weapons.

◄ **Mystery trip?**
At Lindholm Høje in Jutland, Denmark, an extensive Viking cemetery has been uncovered. Many burial sites were marked by stone settings in the shape of a ship. There are about 200 at Lindholm Høje. The use of the ship settings probably means that the Vikings thought of death as a voyage into the unknown.

Viking families and friends liked to preserve this "good name" on huge memorial stones, describing the achievements of the person who had died. Many of these stones, carved with runes and decorated with beautiful designs, have survived until today. Some record ordinary people, like the young girl Astrid, who died around 1040, lovingly remembered by her mother as "the most nimble-fingered girl in Hadeland (Norway)." Others, like a stone found in Sweden, commemorate two brothers, "the best of men, at home and abroad on expeditions."

▶ **Plundered treasure**
This little figure was found decorating a bucket handle in the rich ship-burial at Oseberg in Norway, where a Viking princess was buried. It is believed to have come from Ireland, and been carried back as loot from a Viking pirate raid. It is just one of many beautiful objects buried alongside the dead princess, for her to use in the next world.

Funeral customs

Evidence from Viking graves tells us that the Vikings believed there would be some sort of life after death. But funeral customs differed. In some areas, men and women were buried, along with their most valuable possessions, and, occasionally, their horses, dogs, and slaves. They would need all these things in their future lives. Often they were buried in ships, or within a ring of stones arranged in a boat-shaped pattern. The ship would ferry their spirit to the next world.

Elsewhere, Vikings were cremated. People said their souls would fly to join the gods as the flames rose in the sky. In many places, the Vikings made family burial grounds close to their farms. Their dead ancestors could watch over living family members—and perhaps come back to haunt them, or to cause mischief.

CHRISTIAN KINGS

Although the Vikings all spoke the same language, the *donsk tunga* (Danish tongue), the Viking lands were never a single kingdom. Local customs and loyalties were too strong. Men and women considered their families first, then their community, and only then their local lords. They may not have thought about nationality at all.

Boundaries between Viking countries were uncertain. If a king was shrewd and powerful, he could control a vast territory through alliances and war. But when he died, his kingdom could easily split up, unless the ruler who followed him was equally strong. In the tenth and eleventh centuries, Viking kings did become stronger. They made new, national laws, appointed many royal officials, and weakened the powers of local lords. Slowly, in this

▶ **Two faiths**
The Gosforth Cross, from northwest England. It is decorated with Christian and pagan patterns, influenced by Viking designs.

"WATERFALL OF THE GODS"

Godafoss, in Iceland, became famous because the Icelander, Thorgeir, threw all his pagan Viking statues (probably like the ones on pages 44 and 45) into the raging waters when he became a Christian around AD 1000. Thorgeir's dramatic gesture suggests that he was an enthusiastic convert to his new faith.

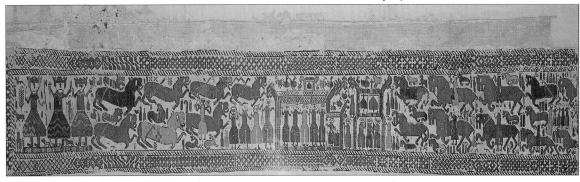

▶ Battling beliefs

This twelfth-century tapestry came from a church at Skog in Sweden. It is believed to show a battle between the pagan Viking gods Odin, Thor, and Frey (left) and Christian people (right). The Christians are ringing the church bells in the belief that loud noises could drive away evil spirits.

way, the three separate kingdoms of Norway, Denmark, and Sweden were formed.

The start of Christianity

From AD 830, Christian missionaries traveled to Viking lands. Some were welcomed; a few were killed. But Viking settlers in England and France soon learned about Christianity from people living there. Many became *prime-signed* (blessed with the cross), so they would be allowed to trade freely with Christian merchants.

The Danes were the first Viking people to become Christian, encouraged by King Harald Bluetooth, who came to power around AD 940. Fifty years later, King Olaf Tryggvason of Norway also decided to introduce Christianity to his lands. Few people dared to disobey Olaf, but in Sweden it took 300 years for people to forget their old pagan gods.

◀ An early church

Stave churches housed the first Christian congregations in Norway. This stave church dates from around AD 1300.

▼ A sign of Christianity

This crucifix from the eleventh century was found in Sweden. It shows that some Swedish people had become Christian.

VIKING TIME CHART

This time chart looks at the years when the Viking peoples left their homelands in Scandinavia to make raids, explore, and found settlements in many distant lands. Between AD 800–1100, Viking skills, customs, beliefs, and vocabulary came to play a vital part in shaping northern European civilization, and in forming the English language that is spoken worldwide today.

VIKINGS AND NEIGHBORS

The Vikings came from cold northern lands on the fringes of Europe. They lived at a time when new civilizations and beliefs were beginning to emerge from the Dark

AD	800	850	900

Swedish soldiers conquer lands in Finland and on the eastern shores of the Baltic Sea.

Viking raiders first sighted off England. They land in Dorset, and kill an English official.

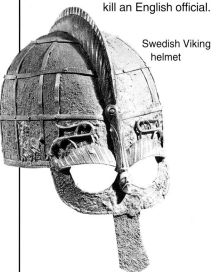

Swedish Viking helmet

Carving of Viking warriors from Lindisfarne

Viking peoples grew powerful. Viking raids on Britain and other lands in northern Europe—France, Netherlands, Ireland, Spain.

French king paid Viking invaders large sums of money not to attack. This encouraged them to come back for more.

Vikings land in Orkney and Iceland; the start of new settlements there.

Viking traders and adventurers traveled in Russia. Set up new trading cities there. They also made long journeys overland to trade with merchants traveling north from the wealthy city of Byzantium (Istanbul) and from Middle Eastern lands.

Great Danish army invaded Britain. Viking settlers occupy eastern England. Viking kingdom based at York.

Viking raiders sailed as far as the Mediterranean, and attacked towns and cities there.

Viking sword

Vikings (Northmen) settled in Normandy, France, and set up an independent state there.

In the Viking homelands, there was fighting between Danes and Norwegians, Germans and Swedes. For a while, Viking raids on other parts of Europe were halted.

Viking sailors traveled to Greenland. Although it is an icy, rocky land, they gave it a pleasant name to encourage other Vikings to settle there.

AROUND THE WORLD

King Offa rules strong Saxon kingdom of Mercia in England.

Muslims rule in Spain.

King Charlemagne of France crowned Holy Roman emperor in Rome. He aimed to set up a mighty new empire in Europe.

Time of great artistic achievements in Japan—stories, paintings, and poetry.

Collapse of Mayan empire in Central America.

Independent Muslim state founded in Spain; became a great center of art and learning.

Ages—the centuries of lawlessness and confusion that followed the break up of the old Roman Empire. Viking peoples fought and traded alongside these developing powers.

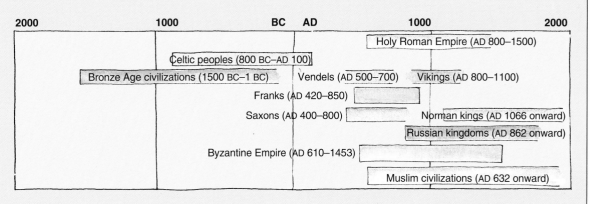

2000	1000	BC	AD	1000	2000

Holy Roman Empire (AD 800–1500)

Celtic peoples (800 BC–AD 100)

Bronze Age civilizations (1500 BC–1 BC)   Vendels (AD 500–700)   Vikings (AD 800–1100)

Franks (AD 420–850)

Saxons (AD 400–800)   Norman kings (AD 1066 onward)

Russian kingdoms (AD 862 onward)

Byzantine Empire (AD 610–1453)

Muslim civilizations (AD 632 onward)

950	1000	1050	1100

Viking raids began again. Vikings invaded Ireland, and attacked city of London in England.

Danish king Harald Bluetooth conquered Norway, and ruled over a large, strong kingdom. From now on, Viking kings began to make new laws, to collect new taxes, and to keep closer control of their kingdoms.

King Harald's memorial stone

King Cnut the Great ruled over a great northern empire, including Norway, Denmark, and parts of Britain.

Viking sailors reached North America. Later, Vikings attempted to settle there, but left after fights with Native American peoples.

Christian missionaries preached in Viking lands. Icelanders voted to adopt Christian beliefs. In other Viking lands, it took over 100 years before the old pagan beliefs were abandoned. Even then, they were not forgotten.

1066 Normans (descendants of the Vikings settled in France) successfully invaded England. Their leader, William, became king.

Last Viking attacks on England. An invading army from Denmark was defeated.

Crucifix from the 11th century found in Sweden

Viking power began to collapse. There were no more Viking raids in Europe.

Christianity spread throughout the Viking homelands.

Viking language, art, and traditions continued to influence writers and artists in many lands where the Vikings settled.

End of attacks by Magyars (nomadic people) in eastern Europe.

Beginnings of Inca state in South America.

"Golden age" of painting and pottery in China.

Beginnings of settlement at Great Zimbabwe, Africa.

Mahmud of Chazni established powerful Muslim state in India.

First Crusade launched by Christian armies against Muslim rulers of the Holy Land.

Great city of Tula built by the Toltec people in Mexico.

First universities established in Europe.

GLOSSARY

(Note: Words in *italics* refer to other entries in the Glossary.)

Ancestors Past members of a family—grandparents, great-grandparents and people who lived even further back in time.

Archaeologist Someone who investigates past civilizations by studying the objects they have left behind them, such as buildings, pottery, bones, metalwork, and all kinds of "treasures."

Armor Strong outer clothing, usually made of leather or metal, worn to protect soldiers in battle. Armor acted like a tough shell, to prevent men from being injured by enemy weapons.

Barter A way of trading, by exchanging goods for others of similar value. If goods were bartered, money was not needed.

Boss Strong metal decoration—usually shaped like a circle—in the middle of a shield.

Cesspit A deep pit where rubbish and sewage were thrown. *Archaeologists* study bones and seeds preserved in ancient cesspits to discover what kinds of animals and plants people ate many centuries ago.

Chariot A small, light, fast cart, pulled by horses, in which people traveled. Often it had only two wheels.

Chronicler Someone who preserves a record of people and events by writing down a description of things as they happen. Chronicles surviving from the past provide us with valuable evidence about life long ago.

Civil Service A group of well-trained people who work for the government. In Viking times, civil servants and clergymen were often the only people who could read and write.

Colony A settlement established in a new area by people coming from a distant land. They run the colony for their own benefit, or to benefit their homeland, without any consideration for the needs of local people.

Community A group of people who share common interests, needs, or concerns. Some communities are based on where people live. Others are based on activities, for example, farming, or on shared interests, such as sport. In Viking times, a community usually included all those people living in one area of

land, who attended the same Thing. Community members often helped one another in times of need.

Democracy A system of government where all people are allowed to share in decision-making, usually by voting to decide on certain policies, or to elect certain leaders.

Duel A fight between two people.

Excavation An investigation into the past made by *archaeologists*. They dig down into the earth to uncover the remains of houses, roads, farms, workshops, and burial places of people who lived long ago. Sometimes also called a dig.

Famine Extreme shortage of food. In Viking times, cold, wet summers or long, snowy winters could cause famines.

Fertile Able to grow good crops.

Feud A war between two families or two rival groups of people.

Fragment A small piece.

Gridiron A flat metal plate, which could be placed close to a fire and used to cook meat.

Hide The skin of animals, treated to make leather. The Vikings used the hides of oxen, cows, goats, and pigs.

Historian Someone who investigates the past, usually, although not always, by studying written evidence, such as chronicles, law-codes, and carved inscriptions (writing on wood and stone).

Hull The body of a ship; the part that floats in the water.

Ivory A smooth, white, shiny substance, taken from the long teeth (tusks) of big animals such as elephants or walruses.

Keel The strong bottom of a boat.

Kingdom The lands ruled by a king, where he makes the laws, collects the taxes, and (in Viking times) led soldiers into battle.

Lances Long, strong spears.

Legend An ancient story, passed down from fathers and mothers to sons and daughters. Many legends record past events, such as the founding of a *kingdom*. Others try to explain religious beliefs. Legends often change over time, as new storytellers add fresh details. Some legends contain true stories, others are mostly make-believe.

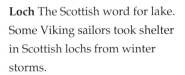

Loch The Scottish word for lake. Some Viking sailors took shelter in Scottish lochs from winter storms.

Loom A simple machine used to weave cloth. You can see a drawing of a loom on page 40.

Loot Valuable goods or money stolen in a Viking pirate raid.

Mast A tall pole in the center of a ship, where the sails are hung.

Memorial Something that helps us remember people who are dead, and their achievements.

Migrate To travel from your homeland to a new place, in search of better conditions, or in the hope of making your fortune.

Missionary Someone who travels to a distant land to spread the teachings of his or her religion to people who follow a different faith, or who have no religious beliefs at all.

Monastery A place where *monks* live.

Monks Men who live together, apart from the rest of the world, because they have devoted their lives to worshiping God.

Myth An ancient story about gods and heroes.

Pagan People who do not believe in the Christian God or in one of the other great faiths of the world, such as Judaism, Islam, Hinduism, or Buddhism. This word is not usually used to describe people today. It is more often used to talk about people in the past.

Pilgrimage A journey to a holy place.

Political intrigue Plots and schemes designed to win power, or to make the leaders you support successful in getting their own way.

Prow The front end of a ship. Viking ships' prows were often decorated with snarling animal heads.

Raid A surprise attack.

Rigging The ropes on a ship that hold the mast and sails in place.

Rune A type of lettering, used by Viking people, to carve messages on wood and stone.

Runic A word used to describe something written in *runes*, or decorated with them.

Scholar Someone who studies hard, and who has learned a lot.

Smithy Place where a blacksmith works.

Soapstone A soft kind of stone, which can be easily carved. The Vikings used it to make bowls and dishes.

Stallion An adult male horse.

Stern The back end of a boat.

Tapestry A cloth woven (or occasionally embroidered) with lots of pictures. Vikings used tapestries woven with pictures of men and women, animals, and gods, to decorate the halls where they held their feasts. Some tapestries dating from the end of the Viking period still survive today.

Taxes Money collected by a government to pay for essential public services, such as an army and a *civil service*.

Textiles A word used to describe all kinds of cloth. Viking textiles included thick woolen cloth used for cloaks, and fine linen cloth used for women's shifts (long, loose dresses, worn next to the skin).

Traditions Customs or beliefs that have survived for many centuries, and which are respected because they are old.

Tunic Clothing worn by men, rather like a very short, straight dress with sleeves. Viking men wore tunics on top of loose shirts to keep themselves warm. They also wore trousers, boots, and cloaks.

Turf Thick slabs of earth with grass growing in it, used to cover the wall frames of Viking houses in Iceland and Greenland.

Warrior A soldier who spends much of his life fighting or preparing for war.

Wattle and daub A mixture of strong twigs, straw, animal hair, and clay, used for building. The wattles (twigs) are woven into a crisscross framework and then covered with the daub (clay). Wattle and daub walls are not as strong as walls made from stone, *turf*, or solid planks of wood.

Worship Saying prayers and singing hymns or chanting so as to praise or give thanks to the gods, or else to ask them for blessings.

INDEX

(Page numbers in *italics* refer to illustrations and captions.)